Poetic Caresses
By: J.D. Garrett

Poetic Caresses   J.D. Garrett

© 2008 by J.D. Garrett.

All rights reserved. No part of this document may be reproduced or transmitted in any form or by any means, electronic, mechanical, photocopying, recording, or otherwise, without prior written permission of J.D. Garrett.

Published in Cornelius, Oregon, by Jaunita D. Garrett

ISBN
978-0-6151-9365-6

Printed in the United States of America

This book is dedicated to my two beautiful daughters, Mariah and Jessica, as well as my friends, family and husband, John.

Table of Contents

Purpose *6*
Bliss *7*
Heart Over Mind *8*
I Understand Now *9*
Of Divine *10*
Perfect World *11*
Seasons *12*
Smile *13*
Somehow the Fates *14*
Time *15*
Wondrous Love *16*
You Are… *17*
Ode To The Computer Age *18*
The Mind *19*
My Own Mind *20*
Trip the Dance *21*
Searching *22*
Fly With Me *23*
Drought *24*
Tree *25*
Distant Land *26*
Needs *27*
Morning Cartoons *28*
Sun's Embrace *29*
Sometimes *30*
Redeem Me *31*
Nature *32*
Please Take My Hand *33*
Rain *34*
Fading Faith *35*
Perspective *36*
A World Apart *37*
Wings *38*
Spirit Me Away *39*
Future Memories *40*
Chrysalis *41*

Imagine *42*
Hear Me! *43*
Erudite Word *44*
The Poet's Soul *45*
The Silence *46*
To Just Say That I Love You *47*
I'll Follow *48*
Please Take My Hand *49*
The Storm *50*
World of Wonder *51*
Follow Me *52*
Everything *53*
Abyss *54*

Purpose

A moment found in time and space
The knowing look upon your face
The second when all is revealed
Of futures past and selves concealed

The knowing instant in your eyes
The reservation in your sighs
The insight that we else would lack
The many times we have looked back

After the floodgates have run dry
That moment that you answer 'why?'
That time when we finally see
What is that is and why should be

The true instant of clarity
Throughout our lives we all do seek
No longer questioning the lack
The simple answers for which we ask

That moment when we look ahead
And know, at last, where life has lead
And in that instant, in that sigh
We finally know it is all right

The jumbled mess that we call life
It has a purpose for our time
And every choice we choose to make
Will inevitably take

Us to the moment when we see
When we truly can believe
There is a purpose to it all
A plan to which we all are called

Bliss

Transport me to the place of dreams
Envision new realities
I've lost the weights and gained my wings
This is the brand new way of things

A time of safety and of peace
Duration of seems not to cease
My woes and fears are now at ease
This bliss my altered state of being

My past was way too circumspect
Was too afraid to jump, and yet
I longed to feel true happiness
Stifled by pain and my regrets

Now I have learned that I can live
I have so very much to give
Finally I can begin
The life I lost I now can win

I only knew my greatest wish
For once to feel true happiness
Was unaware of what I missed
Until you filled my life with bliss

Heart Over Mind

*Sometimes the heart must
Rule the mind
Sometimes the mind is wrong
Sometimes the mind says
"Give it up,"
That's when the heart
Holds strong
Some people say
"Mind conquers all"
"Mind over matter"
Is their battle call
But I see it quite the other way
The heart holds true
When the mind will stray
So when life gets
A little tough
Stay true to your heart
When your mind's given up...*

I Understand Now

*I understand now, it was You
The One that my soul belongs to
I thought I knew but could not see
Just what it meant for You to bleed*

*I've heard the words, I've read Your voice
Sometimes it takes more than just choice
To SEE it, is to truly know
Now I can't help but feel it SO*

*Oh, how You suffered, how You bled
Such painful steps You slowly tread
I cry for how You suffered now
To be Your child, I am proud*

*But shamed to know I shed Your blood
Not just in droplets but a flood
For I'm as guilty as are they
So many times I, too, have strayed*

*Forgive me, Lord, for I have sinned
My thoughts betrayed you deep within
Sometimes it's just so hard to see
You truly shed your blood for me*

Of Divine

Tell me now, I do not know
Towards what destiny I flow
I meander through my days
Knowing not fate's winsome ways

What threads of futures' rope I bare
Do I question? Do I dare?
Or do I meagerly abide
The hidden forces at my side?

Do I dare philosophize
The ebb and flow of it's great tide?
The forces which some take on faith
Yet others argue in their haste

The equation lost to time
Eternal questions of Divine
Could it be the answer's cast
Purposefully beyond our grasp?

<u>Perfect World</u>

*In a perfect world we all are free
No hiding who we wish to be
There are no masks or false "hellos"
We all go where we wish to go*

*No restraints to taint our hearts
No need to lie and keep up guards
We all are free to love and feel
Without the fear that it's not real*

*In this world of which I speak
We all have the love we seek
No one is hurting and alone
We all have families we call home*

*When I slip into my dreams at night
It's in this world that I reside
We all are there and finally see
The love and trust we've been missing*

*So hold my hands and come with me
There is a place that you must see
A place without an unfilled need
A place where true hearts can be free*

*I wish to share this world with you
The souls that my heart belongs to
It is a wonder to behold
Just take my hands, watch it unfold*

Seasons

*Winter, Spring, Summer, Fall
We've been together through it all
Whether the conditions just outside
Or the seasons of our lives*

*Be it cold and dark or sweet sunshine
We've remained friends over the time
We've seen the highs and the down-falls
We've been the one the other called*

*No matter what the circumstance
Our friendship's survived fate and chance
We've had our bitter winter fights
Been the shoulder on which to cry*

*And through the seasons yet to come
Although sparse time seeks it undone
I know our friendship's due to last
For it's been proven in our past*

Smile

The sunset on a cloudy day
The wind that blows your cares away
The blossoms on a tree in spring
The blessings that family brings

The first cry of a newborn child
The first spring day, sunny and mild
The smell on air after a rain
The kiss that takes away the sting

Cozy fire on a cold night
Scoring in a snow ball fight
The rush of loves very first kiss
Joy of a granted birthday wish

The simple things that make your day
That touch you in that special way
That makes the toil worth your while
Are all the things that make you smile

Somehow the Fates

*Somehow the Fates deigned it to be
That on this day would be a Fete
Where two hearts that had beat alone
From this day on would beat as one*

*From separate paths their lives began
They'll merge today, one road to tread
To share the hills; the twists and turns
To grow and love; to live and learn*

*To face the unknown roads ahead
Together held by love they'll tread
To guard each other against cold
To share those secrets once untold*

*And promise, now, unto each one
This bond they make, not be undone
To keep in trust, each other's hearts
Not to let strife render apart*

*This bond, today, we celebrate
Thankful to the reigning Fates
To see the joy of these two souls
Joined today to make each whole*

Time

Time elapses; trepidatingly, excruciatingly
It drips from its continuum to surround us
Forcing us forward, willingly or not
Inexorably toward our future destinies

Like ants in an anthill we march forward
Unaware of the gargantuan forces surrounding us
We trudge through our days, with or without purpose
Lost in our own thoughts, oblivious

Its force absolute, but yet, perspectively variable
Individually crawling by or speeding forward
Caught up in its web we struggle forward
Or are swept unwillingly by its mach force

Invariably we are subjects to its power
Unwittingly at Time's command
Continuously struggling against its iron will
Perpetually caught: until we run out – of time

Wondrous Love

This feeling flooding through my veins
It is so strong I can't refrain
Refrain from speaking out of it
Fearsome my lack will cause it quit

It courses through me as if blood
My heart and soul are over-run
I feel my senses taking leave
Its overwhelming thought and deed

I look upon this love of fire
And feel it burning ever higher
Its embers fed by fuel not seen
Majestic force that of a dream

A heat that has a calming blaze
A wisdom that's an insane craze
A calm that's the eye of the storm
A passion of which comfort's born

With freshness that of morning dew
Each day I find this love renewed
And know that only God above
Could bless me with such wondrous love

<u>You Are...</u>

*You are my home
You are my fire
You are the sum
Of my desire*

*You are my strength
My weakness too
Don't have to hide
When I'm with you*

*You are my waking
Breath each day
You are my sun
When I am gray*

*You are my reason
My defense
With you I need not
Hold pretense*

*You are my shelter
From the rain
You wipe my tears
When I'm in pain*

*You are my smile
Unmasked and free
With you I'm whole
Just being me*

Poetic Caresses   J.D. Garrett

Ode To The Computer Age

*Oh, welcome to
The modern day
Where everything happens
In a technical way
Where the world beyond
Is called cyber space
And everything's viewed
Through an interface!
Where the computer is now
Our best friend
And the only one
Still there in the end
Because we never leave
The computer chair
To take a shower
Or brush our hair!
And if, God forbid,
The power goes down
We'd move to log on
From another town!*

The Mind

My mind is like a flower
Thoughts blooming all about it
Like a tornado ravaging the land
Pictures fold in my mind
Reforming new shapes with different
And wonderful meanings
Dreams encompass me like
The universe about the globe
As I see the vast possibilities
Of unknown intelligence
Dancing around me
I am but a speck of dust
In the sea of reality
But within my own mind
The power is limitless
I explore its depths
With awe and wonder
And just as I reach the peak
Of the mountain that is the mind
I look up and find
That I have climbed only a boulder
That to reach the top
I must continue to climb
Continue to explore
Continue to learn

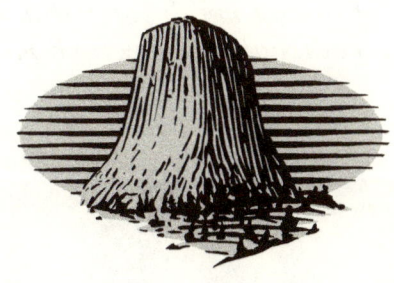

My Own Mind

Pondering the loss of self
One's hopes and dreams placed on a shelf
The sacrifices people make
The chances we're afraid to take

The times we put out lives on hold
Give in until we're numb and cold
The essence lost of who we are
Until our world is torn apart

Then something happens, fate kicks in
We must step back and look within
Examine where our path has lead
See who we've hurt and when we've bled

The introspective time has come
I've learned I can no longer run
I'm walking toward the future now
The walls within are coming down

Seek out the truth and set your goals
Determine what your future holds
Face up to fears your hiding from
To overcome you must not run

It's time; I must rebuild myself
Determination won't be quelled
I'm following my dreams this time
I've rediscovered my own mind

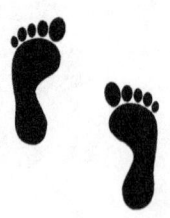

Trip the Dance

Mired in the strains of days
Mores confines me in this cage
Expectations push my bounds
Limits met, essence is drowned

Labor to meet all demands
Caught up short fall to my hands
Cry in outrage at the strain
The tension too much to contain

So-called 'help' a hindrance
Up the tempo, trip the dance
Delivering the writ of ways
As feasible as endless days

Demanding superhuman might
So certain that they know my plight
As seeing as a deafened bat
Their arrogant self-eminence

Searching

*A myriad of paths this
Life leads me to wonder
The endless expanses of
Time I have pondered*

*Searching for something
Too often just squandered
That this world has not
As yet chosen to proffer*

*A light that eludes the
Dark reaches of mind
And illumination of
Soul I must find*

*Pensively groping for
Answers, I've strived
Perhaps in my searching
I have become blind*

*Quite often when I have
Quit looking, I'll see
The item so longed for
Is right before me*

*I've searched for so long
My will is now weak
Perchance if I cease I
Will find what I seek*

Fly With Me

*Fly with me
Join me in the clouds
High above the sea
We'll soar over the land
And through the trees
Through the mountain tops
Where only birds can see*

*Fly with me
You may hold my hand
As you hold my heart
We'll fly over the land
We'll see all the things
Only God can see
While you fly with me*

*Fly with me
Through this life as one
High above the sea
If you will take my hand
As you hold my heart
And just fly with me*

Drought

The branch that snaps off in the breeze
The storm that carries it with ease
The tree so brittle, worn and dry
Winds decimate it each dark night

It's been through times of drought and rain
Knowing it would bloom again
The droughts, they leave it brittle; old
The rains renew, inspire growth

In times of drought it's hard to see
To have faith in what the future brings
Will the tree become a hollow shell?
Without the rains, its thirst to quell?

How long will this new drought last
Before the rain can see it past
The tree to soak up blessed rain
To sprout new leaves and grow again

Tree

*Let me tell you 'bout this flower
That was once sickly and blue
Just could not seem to live up to
All that life had put it through*

*Its petals were all wilted
Its stem a graying stalk
The sun just seemed to miss it
Nor did it get raindrops*

*All of the other flowers
They seemed to shy away
'Cause none of them quite understood
Why it was blue and gray*

*One day a tree was planted
It rose above them all
Reflected down the sunlight
Let flow drops of rainfall*

*And do you know that flower
That was so blue and gray
Grew strong and bright and vibrant
Since that tree came its way*

*My love, I am that flower
You are the giving tree
Before you I was dying
Your love and strength saved me*

Distant Land

Gentle waves ripple softly
Crest and break against me
Enveloping me
In their warm embrace
A slight breeze of uncertainty
Sends shivers up my spine
A moment's lapse
In the warm tide
Allowing the breeze its touch
Quickly the wind of uncertainty
Passes...
Again I am drawn into the waves
Softly held in their grasp
Comforted by their warmth
The newness of the waters
From a far Sea
Beckoning to me
Ever so sweetly
Drawing me out
Teaching me the wonders
Of a distant land...

Needs

I need somebody here by me
I need a love that I can see
I need a lover I can touch
I'm not asking all that much

I need to make some sacrifice
Will the result be worth the price?
I need to take some course of action
One both heart and mind can fathom

I need a fountain for my tears
A bucket to contain my fears
I need someone to make me smile
Someone to go that extra mile

I need your body against mine
A lover's touch sweet and divine
I need someone who can be true
But, mostly, what I need is you

Morning Cartoons

*Little footsteps
Down the hall
Wake us at the
Break of dawn
At the timid knock
You say "come in"
And you have to smile
At her morning grin
"Daddy, can I come
Lay by you?"
You grumble a bit
But you always make room
I turn the TV on
To morning cartoons
And blow you both kisses
As I leave the room*

Sun's Embrace

See the flowers, see the trees
Feel the grass beneath my feet
Feel the warm sun on my face
Scent of wind is filled with grace

Softness of its sweet caress
It's tenderness I'll not forget
Knowing that this Spring will last
Circumventing my torn past

The warmth of this sun will not fade
Forever I'll bathe in its rays
Judge me not its warmth is sweet
Enfolding warmth that brings me peace

Light laughter I glean from its rays
Here I could live for all my days
Knowing it's warmth will never leave
It fills my heart, my soul, my needs

I smile upon its sweet face
And know I've finally found my place
Enfolded in its warming rays
Its here I'll stay for all my days

Sometimes

*Never try and understand
The way that life unfolds
No one ever really knows
Just what the future holds*

*Sometimes you get a glimmer of
The way things could have been
But rarely does the future hold
Those things we dare to dream*

*Sometimes the bitter hand of Fate
Must give your life a twist
Sometimes the hero walks away
Before that final kiss*

*Every "Once upon a time,"
Fate's brother, Irony, takes hold
And life shows what love could have been
Before they broke the mold*

Redeem Me

Won't you take me from this place?
Redeem me from this dark disgrace
Renew my life, redeem my soul
Return my broken heart to whole

I search for balance; find a void
Nothing fills it that I've tried
Digging deeper for the cause
The reason I keep getting lost

Coming up empty I ask you
Why is it I keep going through
This broken cycle to disgrace
Full of things I cannot face

Help me; tell me what to do
How to combat what I'm going through
The answer's eluding, I can't see
I need you to come and redeem me

Nature

The sun fades beyond the trees
Leaving behind
A painted sky
And painted memories
A breeze blows softly
Whistling its tune
As would a guardian angel
Watching over me
The crickets sing
Their midnight song
As the sky darkens
Spreading a peaceful feeling
Across the land
Morning dew caresses
The leaves and the grass
Cackling its joy as the sun
Begins its awakening
With an array of colors
On the freshly prepared canvas
Of nature...

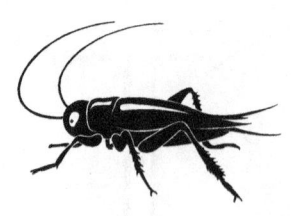

Please Take My Hand

My mind wonders through a dream
Where it leads remains to be seen
I drift alone, a cast away
I don't belong, but yet, I stay

I feel as though my life's on hold
The world around me continues to flow
But still I only stand and stare
My feet refuse, I go nowhere

Won't someone come and take my hand?
Lead me to that Promise Land?
My God takes hold, he leads the way
But still I stumble and forget to pray

Again, my life grinds to a halt
They said, "It's so easy" it isn't my fault
If only I would trust in You
To show me what I am to do

"Please, take my hand, just one more time?"
I may stumble, I may fall
But if you'll only lead the way
This time, I won't forget to pray

Rain

Rain falling all around me
Washing clean the land
Dancing, turning, round and round
Holding out my hands

Washing all the tears away
Bringing out the sun
Children dashing everywhere
Laughing, having fun

Lovers, walking hand in hand
Rain splashing at their toes
A rainbow creeps beyond the trees
Where from nobody knows

Maybe it's a sign from God
For all the world to see
To show us through it's beauty
That He's there for you and me

Fading Faith

I walk along a desert road
At midnight, Dusk, and Dawn
Pictures passing from my life
Show where I've gone wrong

I ask forgiveness for my sins
But yet, I sin again
I plead for guidance in my life
And ask where You have been

I believe in you, to this I swear
But do you believe in me?
Sometimes I ask for your advice
Why don't you answer me?

Its times like this, I ask myself
"Do You really exist?"
If you do, please show some sign
My faith is fading fast

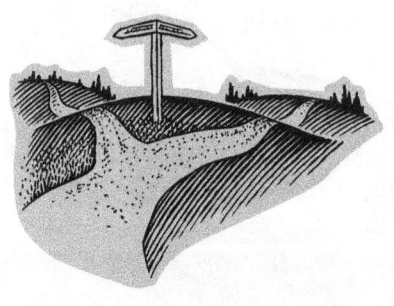

Perspective

Tomorrow is just a dream away
Let rest your sorrows for today
Let each new dawn bring you new hope
And new found means with which to cope

The idle time that comes to pass
A gift of peace that's come at last
In that peace, perspective find
With which to view the rest of time

Those things we thought not of each day
Are now longed for in sad dismay
Thought rightly ours as air to breath
New perspective appreciation breeds

So, next when life has got your down
Let perspective take away that frown
Take not for granted things you have
Let changed perspective light your path

A World Apart

I'll meet you in the world apart
Where we can tread on air
We'll role together in the clouds
The casual heart beware

For ours is not a passing lust
It's embers burn much longer
We're slow and sweet, we burn for life
So casual hearts don't wonder

A touch that's tender as the clouds
As lasting as the sun
Our bodies meld so perfectly
We might as well be one

Just close your eyes, they are the gate
I won't be far behind
There is no distance that's too great
For we'll meet in our minds

Our souls are linked, our hearts are one
There is no time to wait
I'll meet you in a world apart
On the far side of the gates

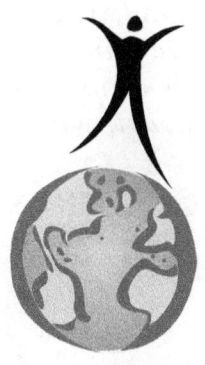

Wings

*Gently, now, I run with you
Together through a sky of blue
I stumble then I seek you out
You reach to me from through the clouds*

*You turn; I see you've sprouted wings
You take them off give them to me
"No longer will you stumble now"
You say as I fly from the ground*

*I see a problem as I float on air
I fly above, but you're stuck down there
The current grabs me and I forget
Caught up in freedom while I drift*

*The wind dies down and I'm alone
I see you watching from the ground
I shed a tear as I think through
The fact I was lost without you*

*Back on the ground my heart is low
How could I leave you on your own?
I take one wing and give it back
Without us both we both will lack*

*I take your hand; you give a smile
Together we can fly for miles
Apart, neither of us is quite whole
For what's a heart, without it's soul?*

Spirit Me Away

Oh come and spirit me away
Escape my troubles for today
Instead just spend the day with you
For you are my heart's dream come true

Oh come and spirit me away
For in your arms I want to stay
In your embrace is my true home
Without you here I'm so alone

Oh come and spirit me away
We'll dance around the Milky Way
Our audience will be the stars
We'll dance across the stage of Mars

Oh come and spirit me away
For in my heart and mind you stay
No other in this world can be
The answer to my one true need

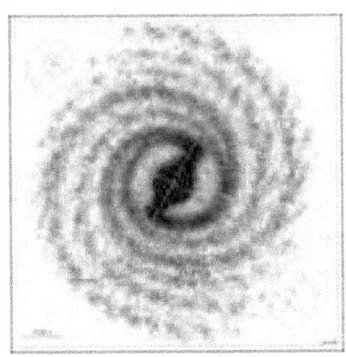

Future Memories

The past is just a memory
The future something I can't see
They say I must live for today
But for today you're far away

And so I reach out from afar
Even if only from my heart
I know somewhere you wait for me
Wait for that future I can't see

I paint the picture in my mind
A place where I spend most my time
It is a wondrous dream I see
This future where you wait for me

We're in a house we call our own
The girls, they play, outside our home
You and I sit in the shade
Talking as they laugh and play

Later on, they're tucked in bed
All our 'good nights' have been said
Soft music wafts throughout the room
And candles keep away the gloom

There we are, just you and I
Talking late into the night
Sharing all our hopes and dreams
Creating future memories

Chrysalis

*Don't tell me what I cannot do
I'll have to prove it wrong to you!
There's so much I have overcome
And I have only just begun!*

*I'm the embodiment of change
My spectrum spreading the full range
I'm colored shades of every hue
I'd love to share them all with you*

*Like the Chrysalis starting out
I've only just begun to sprout
Stay near me and in time you'll see
Eventually I will sprout wings*

*For now this stage has just begun
I'm walking now, but soon I'll run
I ask you, will you run with me?
Then, someday soon, we'll spread our wings*

Imagine

Imagine what the world could be
If only we could live our dreams
A world of wonders and delights
Of fairy tales; fantasy flights

Imagine the life you would choose
The possibilities just ooze
Out of a mind that's full of dreams
A wonderland of things to please

Imagine creatures of such grace
Such beauty from another place
There's endless possibilities
A world made up of fantasies

No ugliness would be allowed
There would be no pain to be found
A wonderful world filled with dreams
Imagined from our fantasies

Hear Me!

Oh, heed now, these angry words
This is a voice that must be heard
These are not thoughts that can be quelled
Nor mine a voice that will be stilled

I will fight you high and low
You think on me you can bestow
Some judgment to which I'll just give
Well, watch now, as the fight begins

You'll not find here some idle mind
Incapable of giving fight
My mind's a gun that's full and cocked
It's aimed at you and will go off

Now you just wait, my aim is good
I say this so we're understood
I will not sit here idly by
As you attempt to take my life

So hear me now and hear me well
I say, again, I won't be quelled
I will fight and I will win
So, get ready, this fight begins

Erudite Word

Oh, these nights will bare me true
They'll strip me to the core and through
I'm weary and my nerves laid raw
I've been backed up against the wall

I am so vexed with commonplace
My patience gone with ne'er a trace
Benighted fools have pushed me here
Sequestered me without a care

And now I'm true; I've been laid bare
There's no façade lingering here
So wary, now, the fools should be
It won't take much to quicken me

I'm forging, now, my vicious sword
Composed of quite erudite word
So if you cannot stand your ground
On that forum then back down now

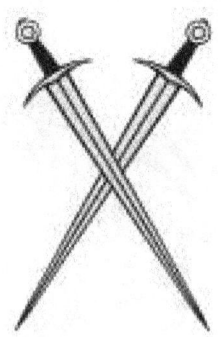

The Poet's Soul

*The tortured soul I know it well
It's angst and sorrow ebbs and swells
Heart beating in its ivory cage
Pounding out its bitter rage*

*The burning cyclone from within
Blazing fire; fury's sin
It casts into cyclonic haze
The ever-present endless maze*

*Caught up in the fury's spell
The joy rides erupt into hell
The sunlight casts it out again
The torrent slowing to a spin*

*The spin cascades into a flow
The Poet's Soul I live and know
The flow a long awaited tease
Before the torrent steals reprieve*

The Silence

It eats away my sanity
It mocks my every thought and deed
It keeps me from the things I need
The Silence

It makes me fear the light of day
Say to the night, "just go away"
Makes life a game I cannot play
The Silence

It breeds a pain I cannot bare
Trembling with uncertain fear
Brings to my eyes that forlorn tear
The Silence

It starves me with the need to know
Crumbles my heart like brittle snow
Takes from my soul that lively glow
Your Silence

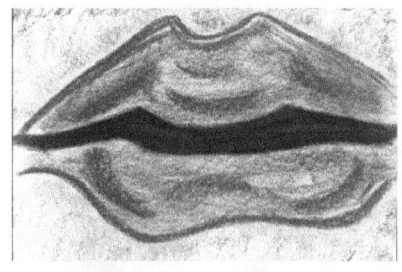

To Just Say That I Love You

To just say that I love you
Would never be enough
I couldn't live without you
And that is not a bluff!

No one in this world
Can seem to understand
In this life I want only you
Together, hand in hand

We were meant to be together
Until eternity
In good and bad, in rich and poor
Together, you and me

So, just to say, "I love you"
Really, will not do
For in this world words don't exist
To say how I love you

I'll Follow

Shall we sing a happy tune,
Together, you and I?
Whistling under the full moon
The stars and midnight sky?
Or shall we let the crickets sing
Lulled by the morning sun?
Their song a tune to wake the world
A song joyous and fun
Maybe we should spend the day
Exploring distant lands
Sailing foreign shorelines
Building castles in the sand
Well, whatever we are doing
There is one thing that I know
Where you go I will follow
Where you go I will go

Please Take My Hand

My mind wonders through a dream
Where it leads remains to be seen
I drift alone, a cast away
I don't belong but, yet, I stay

I feel as though my life's on hold
The world around me continues to flow
But still I only stand and stare
My feet refuse, I go nowhere

Won't someone come and take my hand?
Lead me to that promise land?
My God takes hold, He leads the way
But still I stumble and forget to pray

Again my life grinds to a halt
They said, "It's so easy," it isn't my fault
If only I would trust in you
To show me what I am to do

Please take my hand just one more time?
I my stumble, I may fall
But if you only guide the way
This time I won't forget to pray

The Storm

A burst of lightening
Ripples across the sky
Followed closely by
The boom of thunder

Suddenly, all is silent
The land holds its breath
In trembling anticipation

Black clouds cover the horizon
And the freezing downpour begins

The tornado appears with a fury
Whipping along quickly
It ravages everything in its path

As quickly as it began it is over
The clouds are replaced
By the warmth of the sun
And the healing begins

World of Wonder

In a world unknown to time
A land known only in my mind
A land where all my dreams come true
A place where I can be with you
A world of beauty and desire
Sunlit beaches and bonfires
Where pain and fear are yet unknown
A world of wonder all my own
It is this place I travel to
When I dream of a life with you

Follow Me

Close your eyes
And follow me
I am your heart
I'll set you free

I'll tell you what
Is right from wrong
I'll hold you up
And make you strong

I'll tell you when
You are in danger
Those times when you
Can trust a stranger

I am the ruler
Of your dreams
I am the source
Of your instincts

So, follow me
And hold on tight
It isn't me
You need to fight

Just trust me and
I will guide you
I am your heart
I'll lead you true

Everything

You've taught me how to live and love
You've taught me how to care
And when the burden was too much
You taught me how to share

You were my idol as I grew
You showed me right from wrong
And when I tripped along life's path
You taught me to be strong

You taught me I don't have to be
Alone in all I do
And when the burden was too much
You let me lean on you

So, Dad, I just want you to know
How much you mean to me
You've been there for me through it all
You are my everything

Abyss

At my feet is the abyss
I balance at its dismal edge
The wind is harsh against my back
In front of me a blatant lack

The voices call me from below
They echo of a song I know
Behind me I can hear the storm
It screeches with a sound forlorn

I do not see a way across
I'm told it's there but I am lost
They say it's right in front of me
But I am blind and cannot see

The light that once was there to guide
Is gone from me, could not abide
If he gave up then why can't I?
Into the abyss now I cry

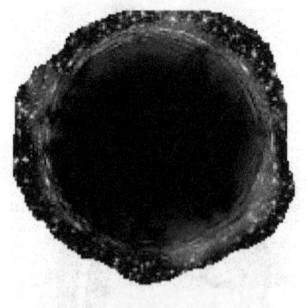

About the Author:

Jaunita D. Garrett

I started writing poetry when I was 18 years old and haven't stopped yet. I derive inspiration from family, friends, life, and the world around me.

www.ingramcontent.com/pod-product-compliance
Lightning Source LLC
Chambersburg PA
CBHW031433040426
42444CB00006B/793